Audrey Hepburn

A Little Golden Book® Biography

By Emily Easton
Illustrated by Ellen Surrey

A GOLDEN BOOK • NEW YORK

Text copyright © 2024 by Emily Easton
Cover art and interior illustrations copyright © 2024 by Ellen Surrey
All rights reserved. Published in the United States by Golden Books, an imprint of
Random House Children's Books, a division of Penguin Random House LLC, 1745 Broadway,
New York, NY 10019. Golden Books, A Golden Book, A Little Golden Book, the G colophon,
and the distinctive gold spine are registered trademarks of Penguin Random House LLC.
rhcbooks.com
Educators and librarians, for a variety of teaching tools, visit us at RHTeachersLibrarians.com
Library of Congress Control Number: 2023938892
ISBN 978-0-593-70332-8 (trade) — ISBN 978-0-593-70333-5 (ebook)
Printed in the United States of America
10 9 8 7 6 5 4 3 2 1

On May 4, 1929, Audrey Kathleen Ruston was born in Brussels, Belgium. It was a surprisingly simple name for the child of Ella van Heemstra, a Dutch baroness, and Joseph Victor Anthony Hepburn-Ruston, who believed he was related to an English earl who had been married to Mary, Queen of Scots.

When Audrey was six years old, her father moved to London.

Her mother saw how sad she was. To cheer her up, she sent Audrey to a boarding school in England to be near him. But Audrey missed her older brothers, and she didn't speak English yet, so it was hard for her to make friends.

Then, when she was eight years old, a dancer came to her school, and Audrey fell in love with ballet! Her world brightened as she took lessons and devoted herself to becoming a ballerina.

But the world around Audrey started falling into darkness. England and Germany were on the brink of war. Audrey's mother got permission for her daughter to leave England, and her father put her on one of the last flights out of London. They thought she would be safe with her mother in Holland.

Unfortunately, World War II soon arrived there, as well. After Germany took over their country in 1940, Audrey and her mother joined their neighbors in the Dutch Resistance, a secret group that fought the Germans in nonviolent ways. Audrey hid coded messages in her shoes and delivered food and notes to English and American pilots hiding in the forest.

Through it all, Audrey's love of ballet gave her hope—and a way to help others. She planned secret dance performances in friends' homes to raise money for the resistance. The audience had to be quiet, and the windows covered. They couldn't risk having enemy soldiers hear clapping or see lights coming from the house. But Audrey and the dancers dazzled their neighbors in homemade felt slippers and tights knitted from yarn scraps.

The last year of the war was the hardest of all.
Audrey's town became a battleground. Her family
had only grass, turnips, and tulips to eat. There
was no more energy for dancing—just survival.

Then, just as hope was fading, the Germans lost the battle. When her family crept out of their cellar, a friendly soldier handed Audrey seven precious chocolate bars. United Nations workers came next, with medicine, blankets, food, and clothing to bring the town back to life.

After the war, Audrey and her mother moved to London so Audrey could be a dancer. Sadly, she discovered she was too tall to be a prima ballerina. And going without healthy food for so long during the war left her weak and frail.

Audrey became an actress instead, getting small parts in British films. One of those movies took her to France. While there, she caught the eye of the legendary French writer Colette, who was casting her new Broadway play *Gigi*.

Colette took one look at Audrey and said, "Voilà! There is my Gigi!"

In New York City, Audrey threw herself into acting lessons and rehearsals. On opening night, she was so terrified that she forgot some of her lines. But the audience loved her—and so did the critics. One reviewer said Audrey was "as fresh and frisky as a puppy out of a tub." She was the toast of Broadway!

As soon as *Gigi* ended, Audrey flew to Italy to act in the movie that would make her a star. In *Roman Holiday,* she plays Princess Ann, who runs away from her royal life and falls in love with a reporter. The role won Audrey an Oscar for Best Actress. The daughter of a Dutch baroness was now Hollywood royalty for playing a princess!

Audrey quickly followed this triumph by winning
a Tony Award for Best Actress for playing a water
sprite in a Broadway play called *Ondine*—a rare
double honor in one year.

Audrey worked hard and challenged herself throughout her long career. Her fans loved watching her transform into so many different characters. From a poor flower seller trying to change her life in *My Fair Lady* to a Russian countess in *War and Peace* to a woman who hires a burglar to steal a fake sculpture in *How to Steal a Million*, Audrey did it all.

While Audrey's acting made her a movie star, French designer Hubert de Givenchy's clothes made her a fashion icon. Givenchy made fancy gowns to give Audrey's character a makeover in *Sabrina*. He used black skinny pants, a black turtleneck, and black flats to show Audrey's free spirit when she danced in *Funny Face*. And she outshined the glitz of New York City in the little black dress and oversized sunglasses she wore in *Breakfast at Tiffany's*. Women wanted to dress just like Audrey! And her style is still beloved today.

After years of making movies, Audrey took time off to be with her sons, Sean and Luca. Her marriages to their fathers didn't last, but she hoped to give them the happy childhood she never had. And she wanted to do the same for children everywhere!

UNICEF had helped Audrey when World War II ended—now it was her turn to help them. She became a UNICEF goodwill ambassador and brought aid to children in danger. Audrey used her star power to draw attention to their needs. And she traveled the world to lend a hand or give a hug.

President George H. W. Bush awarded her the Presidential Medal of Freedom for her tireless charitable work, which she continued until her death on January 20, 1993.

The girl hiding from war in her cellar could never have imagined how far she would travel and all the lives she would change.

Audrey's star still shines bright—for her sons, movie fans, fashionistas, and all the children she helped around the world!

"Nothing is **IMPOSSIBLE.** The word itself says '**I'M POSSIBLE!**'"